ALL ABOUT THINGS PEOPLE DO

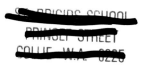
331.7
RIC

Careers

Kingfisher Books, Grisewood & Dempsey Ltd,
Elsley House, 24–30 Great Titchfield Street,
London W1P 7AD

First published in paperback in 1992 by Kingfisher Books
10 9 8 7 6 5 4 3 2 1
Originally published in hardback in 1989 by Kingfisher Books

BRITISH CATALOGUING IN PUBLICATION DATA
A catalogue record for this book is
available from the British Library

ISBN 0 86272 524 0

Edited by Camilla Hallinan
Designed by Penny Mills
Phototypeset by Southern Positives and
Negatives (SPAN), Lingfield, Surrey
Colour separations by Scantrans Pte Ltd, Singapore
Printed in Spain

MELANIE & CHRIS RICE

ALL ABOUT THINGS PEOPLE DO

Illustrated by
Lesley Smith

Kingfisher Books

Contents

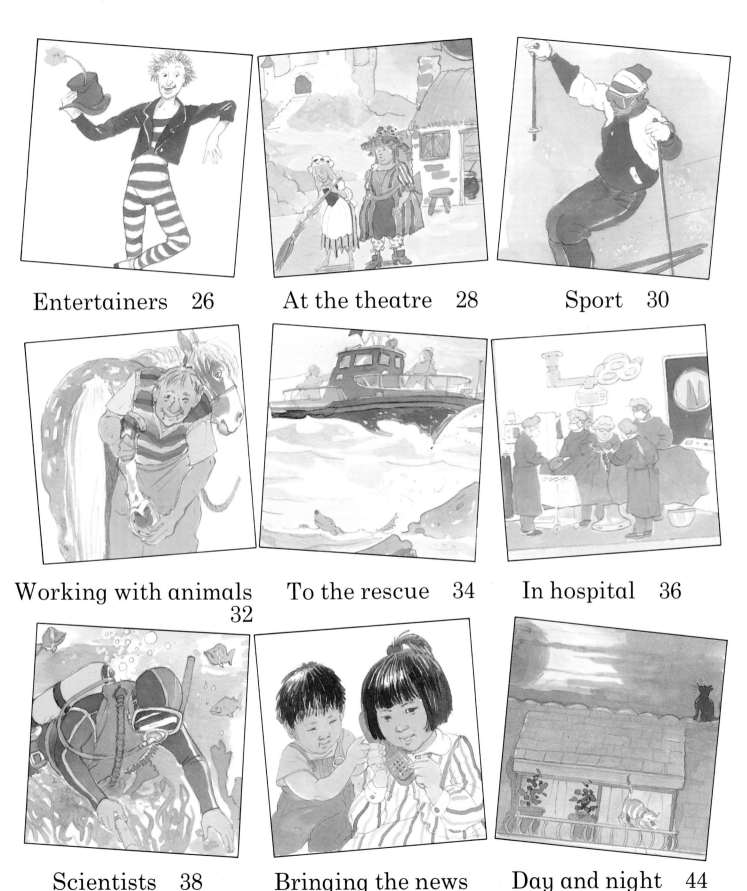

All around

People are busy everywhere, in towns and cities, in the countryside and at sea, even under the ground.

farming

fishing

collecting the rubbish

mining

People are busy at home
and at work . . .

. . . helping out . . .

. . . and having fun.

9

Drivers

Drivers take people and their belongings from one place to another.

taxi driver

bus driver

rickshaw wallah

lorry driver

Here are some of the people who work at an airport.

A ground stewardess checks passenger tickets.

A baggage handler takes suitcases to the plane.

Ground engineers refuel the plane.

pilot

captain

courier

engine driver

gondolier

A flight engineer makes sure the plane is ready to fly.

A stewardess looks after the passengers.

An air traffic controller guides the pilot for take-off.

In the factory

In a car factory people work alongside robots and computers. Each person concentrates on just one part of the assembly line.

1 Before work begins, the design engineer draws up plans and models are tested.

4 The windscreens are sealed in place before the fitters lower the body onto its engine.

5 Then the insides of the car and its wheels are added. At every stage, supervisors check production standards.

2 Fitters position the side panels for the robots to weld together.

3 After the fitters hang the doors and bonnets on their hinges, robots spray the body of the car with paint.

6 Technicians test the car to make sure that everything works perfectly.

7 When people and machines work together, they can produce hundreds of cars each day.

Hands at work

Craftsmen and women, such as this basket weaver, make things by hand. People admire hand-crafted things because they take time and skill to make.

The potter shapes a pot from wet clay on a potter's wheel.

When the pot is dry he hardens it in a hot kiln.

When the pot is cold he decorates it with paint and glaze and fires it again in the kiln.

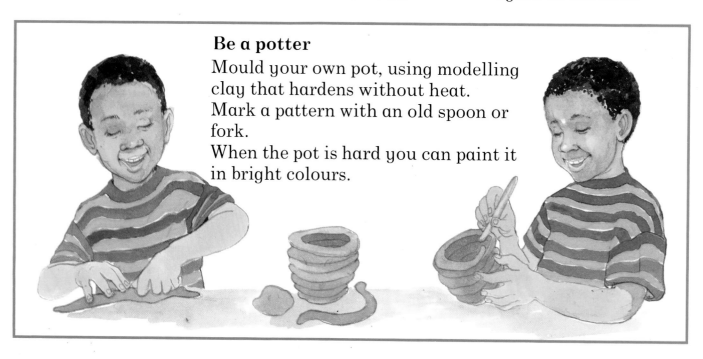

Be a potter

Mould your own pot, using modelling clay that hardens without heat.
Mark a pattern with an old spoon or fork.
When the pot is hard you can paint it in bright colours.

Carpenters cut and join wood using the tools in their workshop.

Glassblowers blow and twist hot glass into shapes which harden as they cool.

This watchmaker is checking tiny parts with a magnifying lens.

Builders

On construction sites many people work together. Before the builders begin, designers, architects and engineers discuss and plan the best way to carry out the job.

Building a tunnel

Building a bridge

Building a road

The designer must make the tunnel strong enough to hold back earth and water.

Engineers make sure the bridge will stand up to wind, waves and heavy traffic.

The surveyor measures the land so that the road will be straight and smooth.

A ship is designed on computers and tested with models before it is built in the shipyard.

Each section is constructed in an assembly hall and rolled out to the building dock.

A crane driver lifts the sections.

A welder joins them together.

A painter sprays over the joins.

Doing repairs

All the things we use, no matter how well they are made, need maintaining to stay in good order. When they break or go wrong they have to be repaired. Have you seen these people at work?

plumber

electrician

painter

window cleaner

road worker

telephone engineer

Mechanics work in a garage, servicing and mending cars.

A tool box

People need all kinds of tools to help them with their work.
Who uses these tools?

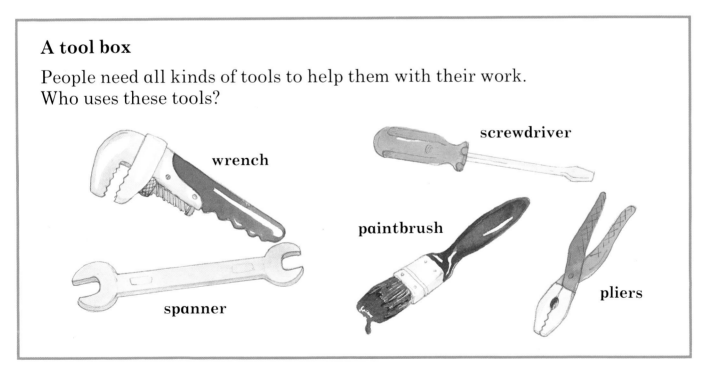

wrench

screwdriver

spanner

paintbrush

pliers

Making clothes

People make clothes at home, in small workshops and factories, by hand and with machines.

machine-made gymshoes

a hand-knitted jumper

a handmade hat

Here are some of the people who produced this cotton T-shirt.

A harvester gathered the cotton.

A spinner spun the cotton into thread.

A knitter wove the threads into material.

20

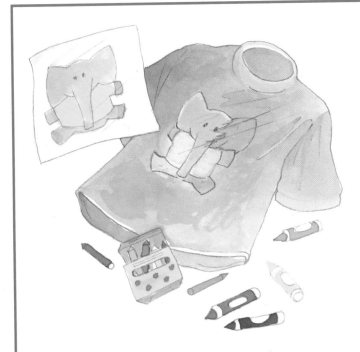

Be a designer

You need some paper, pencils, an old T-shirt and fabric crayons.

Draw your design on a piece of paper. Copy it onto the front of your T-shirt and colour it in with fabric crayons.

Ask an adult to cover the picture with paper or cloth and to iron over it. The heat will fix the colours.

A dyer coloured the material.

A designer sketched the T-shirt.

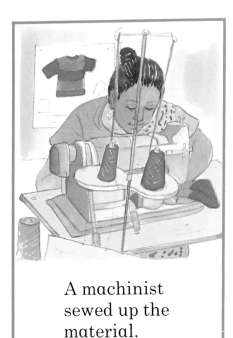

A machinist sewed up the material.

In the shops

We go shopping to buy the things we need. Shop assistants help us to find what we want and take our money at the till. They also fill the shelves and arrange displays.

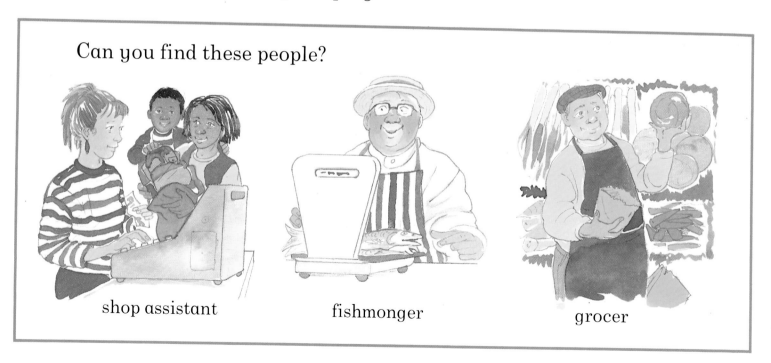

Can you find these people?

shop assistant   fishmonger   grocer

The Hot Bread Shop

HADDOCK & SON

At the hairdresser

Some shops sell services, not goods.

Hairdressers are trained to wash and cut their customers' hair.

The customers choose from the
menu. The chef cooks their meal.

Waiters bring the
food to the table.

24

At the restaurant

People eat at a restaurant when they are too busy to cook their own meals or when they want a treat.

Can you see someone washing up?

You can buy ready-to-eat snacks in the street as well.

American hot-dogs

Italian ice-cream

Nigerian sweetcorn

Entertainers

Entertainers try to make their audience happy. They make them think too. Which entertainers do you enjoy watching most?

clown

magician

singer

musicians

Writers and illustrators entertain us with their books. But we do not watch them at work.

folk dancer

ballet dancers

circus acrobat

At the theatre

People come to the theatre to see the actors and musicians, but others are at work behind the scenes.

The director leads the rehearsals.

The wardrobe mistress sews the costumes.

Scenic artists paint the sets for the stage.

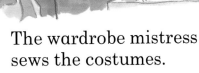

Sound and lighting technicians operate the sound and light effects.

Sport

Sport is enjoyed by people everywhere. Some like to take part, others prefer to watch.

jogging

skiing

sailing

swimming

People compete against each other . . .

basketball

. . . and play together in teams.

athletics

We can watch sport live
and at home on television.

snooker

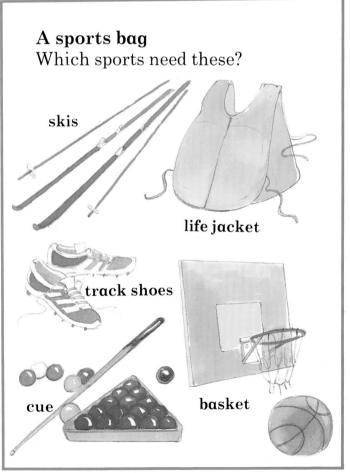

A sports bag
Which sports need these?

skis

life jacket

track shoes

cue

basket

Working with animals

Animals are trained to help people with all kinds of work.

Oxen help a farmer to plough the land.

Guide dogs help blind people.

A team of huskies drags a sledge across the snow.

A camel carries a load across the desert.

An elephant moves heavy timber.

Animals everywhere
need to be cared for.

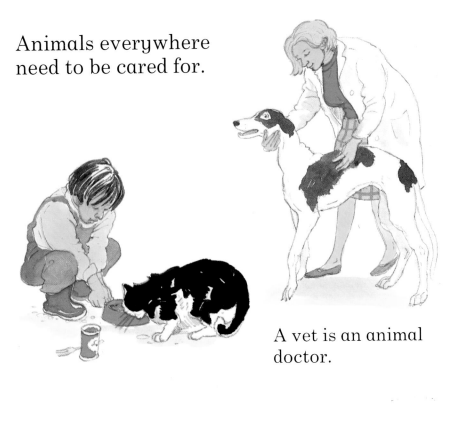

A vet is an animal
doctor.

A farrier shoes horses
and ponies.

Wardens protect wild animals
in parks and nature reserves.

The zookeeper makes sure that his
animals are clean and well fed.

To the rescue

The emergency services help people in danger. Firefighters, ambulance workers and police are hard at work at this fire.

Other people help out too.

health visitor

minister

neighbour

friend

Coastguards have called lifeboat and helicopter crews to the rescue.

In hospital

Day and night, doctors and nurses care for their patients in hospital. Receptionists, porters, cooks and cleaners all work hard behind the scenes.

Ward

Intensive Care Ward

Ward

1

X-ray Room

6

Operating Theatre

3 4

Laboratory

8

Accident & Emergency

10

Reception

9

Children's Ward

5

Special Care Baby Unit

7

Maternity Unit

Canteen

Kitchen

Outpatients

2

Can you find these people in the picture?

1 a nurse

2 a doctor

3 a surgeon in the Operating Theatre

4 a theatre nurse

5 a physiotherapist

6 a radiographer in the X-ray Room

7 a midwife in the Maternity Unit

8 a pharmacist in the Laboratory

9 a telephone operator in Reception

10 an ambulance worker in Accident & Emergency

Scientists

Scientists try to find out more about how our world works. There are many kinds of scientists doing research. They set themselves questions and conduct experiments to test their answers.

Some scientists look for cures for diseases.

Some try to find new ways of growing food.

Some search for clues that tell us more about the past.

Some investigate the sea bed . . .

. . . and some explore remote parts of the world.

Astronauts travel to space in rockets.

They do tests and bring back information which might be useful to us on Earth.

Astronomers study stars in the sky.

Try this experiment
What happens to sugar in water? Add some sugar to a glass of water and stir it.

Watch. The sugar disappears and becomes part of the water. It dissolves.

At school

These children are busy learning with their teachers at school.

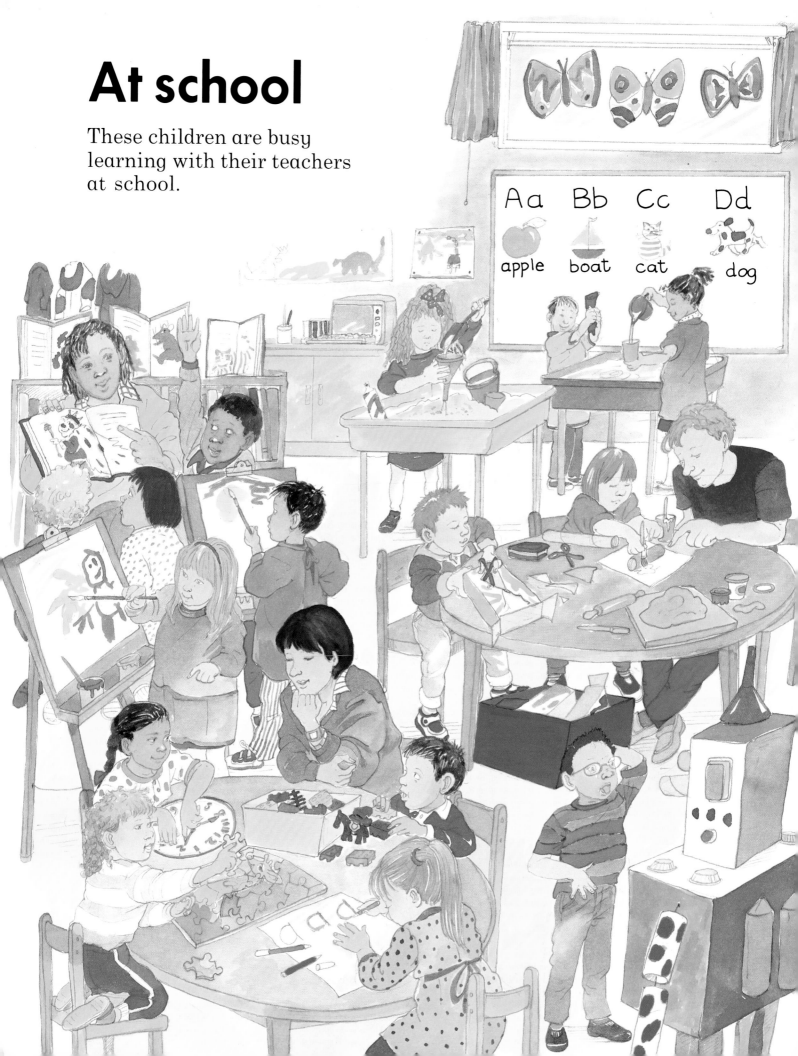

Aa apple
Bb boat
Cc cat
Dd dog

The first people we learn from are our parents. As we grow up, teachers can tell us more about the things that interest us.

music teacher

museum guide

librarian

medical professor

sports trainer

Bringing the news

We can find out what people are doing wherever they are.

We can ask them by making a phone call.

Telephone operators and engineers help us to keep in touch.

They can tell us in a letter or a postcard.

A postman delivers a postcard.

Reporters and photographers go out and meet people. Their stories are printed in newspapers and magazines for us to read.

Film crews travel to make the programmes we watch on television.

Radio presenters broadcast the news and other programmes from their studio.

Busy people day and night

The Corner Shop

10

The Corner Shop

10

CLOSED

Index

MORE KINGFISHER PAPERBACKS FOR YOU TO ENJOY

Also in the All About Series:

ALL ABOUT BABY ANIMALS
ISBN 086272 525 9 £3.50

ALL ABOUT FARM ANIMALS
ISBN 086272 520 8 £3.50

ALL ABOUT DINOSAURS
ISBN 086272 649 2 £3.50

And in the Magic Bus Series:

THE MAGIC BUS AT THE WATERWORKS
ISBN 086272 791 X £2.95

THE MAGIC BUS INSIDE THE HUMAN BODY
ISBN 086272 788 X £2.95

THE MAGIC BUS LOST IN THE SOLAR SYSTEM
ISBN 086272 867 3 £2.99

THE MAGIC BUS INSIDE THE EARTH
ISBN 086272 866 5 £2.99

Kingfisher Books are available from most bookshops or by post from:

KINGFISHER CASH SALES
P.O. BOX 11
FALMOUTH
CORNWALL TR10 9EN

If you wish, you may fax your order to FAX NO: 0326 376423. Please state your name and address and list the titles required.

Payments can be made as follows: Cheque, postal order (payable to Kingfisher Books) or by credit card Visa/Access (Mastercard), stating card number and expiry date.
PLEASE DO NOT SEND CASH OR CURRENCY.

Please include with your payment the following amount for postage and packing:

UK customers (including BFPO):
one book £1.00
second book .... plus £0.50
plus 30p each additional book to a maximum charge of £3.00 (7 books plus)

Overseas (including Eire):
one book £2.00
second book .... plus £1.00
plus 50p each additional book

While every effort is made to keep prices low, prices of books and postage/packing are subject to change without notice. Kingfisher Books reserves the right to show new retail prices on covers that may differ from those previously advertised here or elsewhere.